SPORTS STARTERS

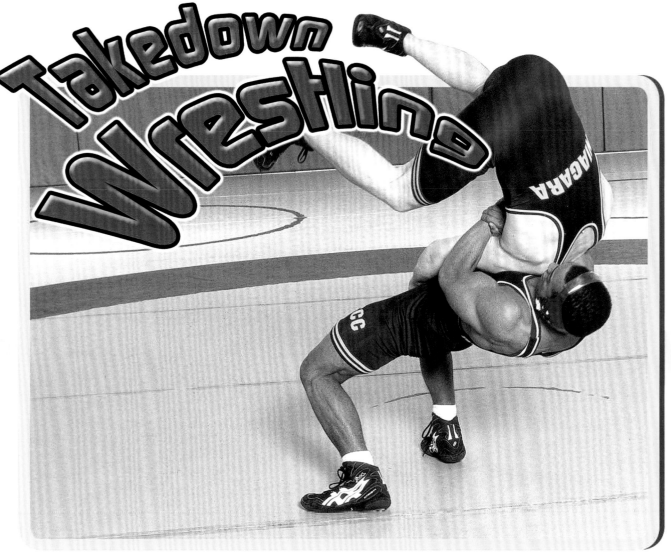

Takedown Wrestling

Robin Johnson

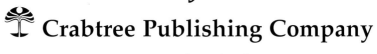

Crabtree Publishing Company

www.crabtreebooks.com

SPORTS STARTERS

Created by Bobbie Kalman

Author
Robin Johnson

Project coordinator
Kathy Middleton

Editor
Lynn Peppas

Photo research
Crystal Sikkens

Design
Margaret Amy Salter

**Production coordinator
and prepress technician**
Margaret Amy Salter

Print coordinator
Katherine Berti

Special thanks to
Sheldon Francis, Josiah Boyd, Victoria McGoldrick, Rebecca Marshall,
Attila Kasap, Howard Leung, Ellen Macro, Courtnay Lafond, Katie Mercer

Illustrations
Bonna Rouse: page 9

Photographs
© Marc Crabtree: pages 1, 5, 7, 10, 11, 14, 16, 17, 19, 21, 22, 23, 24
Dreamstime: page 4; Susan Leggett: page 31
iStockphoto: page 20
Keystone Press: ZUMAPRESS.com: pages 28, 29
Shutterstock: front cover, page 3; max blain: page 6; Susan Leggett:
    back cover, page 30
Wikimedia Commons: Dreier Carr: pages 12, 18, 25; Nam Tran:
    pages 13, 15; JonRidinger: pages 26-27

Library and Archives Canada Cataloguing in Publication

CIP available at Library and Archives Canada

Library of Congress Cataloging-in-Publication Data

Johnson, Robin (Robin R.)
  Takedown wrestling / Robin Johnson.
    p. cm. -- (Sports starters)
  Includes index.
  ISBN 978-0-7787-3155-9 (reinforced library binding : alk. paper) -- ISBN
978-0-7787-3182-5 (pbk. : alk. paper) -- ISBN 978-1-4271-9063-5 (electronic
pdf) -- ISBN 978-1-4271-9117-5 (electronic html)
  1. Wrestling--Takedown--Juvenile literature. I. Title.

  GV1196.4.T33J65 2013
  796.812--dc23
                                        2012035164

Crabtree Publishing Company

Printed in Canada/102012/MA20120817

www.crabtreebooks.com   1-800-387-7650

Published in Canada
Crabtree Publishing
616 Welland Ave.
St. Catharines, Ontario
L2M 5V6

Published in the United States
Crabtree Publishing
PMB 59051
350 Fifth Avenue, 59th Floor
New York, New York 10118

Published in the United Kingdom
Crabtree Publishing
Maritime House
Basin Road North, Hove
BN41 1WR

Published in Australia
Crabtree Publishing
3 Charles Street
Coburg North
VIC 3058

Contents

What is wrestling?   4

Style file   6

On the mat   8

The basics   10

Ready to wrestle!   12

Pin to win   14

Combos and cradles   16

Half nelsons   18

Get the point   20

Takedowns   22

Breaking the rules   24

Meet your match   26

Fighting for gold   28

Flex your muscles   30

Glossary and Index   32

What is wrestling?

Wrestling is a combat, or fighting, sport. Wrestlers face off and try to come out on top. They move, throw, hold, escape, and take each other down. The wrestler who **pins** the other person down to the ground or gets control wins the fight.

The wrestler in red is trying to pin his opponent to win the fight.

A wrestler must be strong and fast and have good balance to win a match.

Face to face

A wrestling competition is called a **match**. In most wrestling matches, two people face off against each other on large mats. They use their whole bodies to try to overpower their **opponents** and hold them down. The wrestlers do not use weapons or try to hurt each other.

Style file

There are hundreds of different wrestling styles used around the world. Each style has its own rules and **techniques**. The main styles used in **international** events are freestyle and Greco-Roman wrestling. Wrestlers compete in these sports at the Olympic Games and in other major events.

Pro wrestling

Professional wrestling is not like other forms of wrestling. Pro wrestlers plan and perform wild stunts to entertain their fans. This type of wrestling is a show, not a sport.

Folkstyle wrestling

Most young wrestlers compete in a type of
freestyle wrestling called folkstyle wrestling.
It takes place in school gyms and wrestling
clubs in the United States and other
countries. This book focuses on the rules
and techniques of folkstyle wrestling.

*Folkstyle wrestling is also
called scholastic wrestling.*

On the mat

Wrestling matches take place on big, thick rubber mats on the floor. A large outer circle is marked on the mats. The circle is at least 28 feet (9 m) across. Wrestlers must stay inside the circle during a match. If they go outside the circle, they are out of bounds.

The inner circle

A smaller inner circle is marked inside the large circle. It is about 10 feet (3 m) across. Wrestlers try to stay inside this small circle so they do not risk going out of bounds. Inside the small circle are two starting lines. The home wrestler starts a match on the green starting line. The visiting wrestler starts on the red starting line.

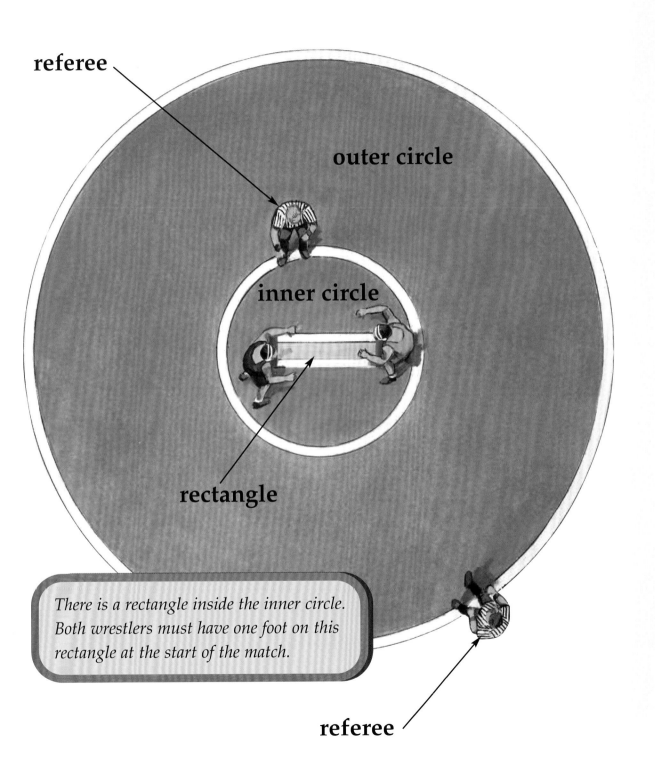

referee

outer circle

inner circle

rectangle

There is a rectangle inside the inner circle. Both wrestlers must have one foot on this rectangle at the start of the match.

referee

The basics

A folkstyle wrestling match is made up of three **periods**. Each period lasts one to three minutes. The length of the periods depends on the age of the wrestlers and the event. Wrestlers fight opponents in the same **weight class**. A small wrestler will never have to face a much heavier opponent.

These girls are in the same weight class. Sometimes they might also wrestle boys who are in the same weight class as them.

Many young wrestlers wear singlets that show their school or team colors.

Suit yourself

Wrestlers who compete wear tight, stretchy, one-piece uniforms called **singlets**. They wear light shoes with rubber bottoms for a good grip on the mats. All young wrestlers must wear headgear to compete in folkstyle wrestling events. Headgear is safety equipment that covers a wrestler's ears. Some wrestlers also wear mouthguards, knee pads, elbow pads, or other gear to keep them safe.

Ready to wrestle!

At the start of a match, two wrestlers face each other in the center of the mat. Each wrestler puts one foot on their own starting line. The wrestlers shake hands. Then the referee blows a whistle, and the match begins! The wrestlers try to throw the other person off balance and bring them down to the mat.

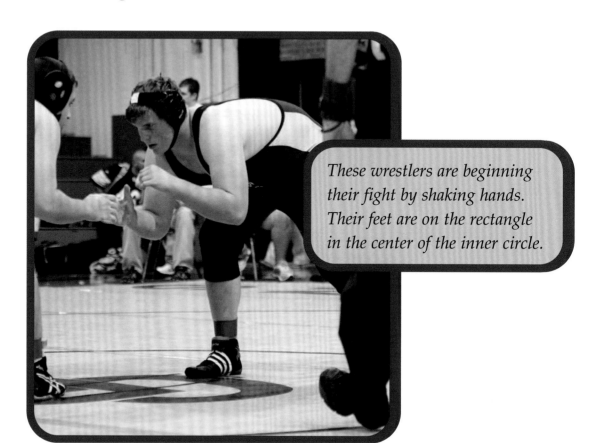

These wrestlers are beginning their fight by shaking hands. Their feet are on the rectangle in the center of the inner circle.

Seconds and thirds

If no one wins in the first period, the match continues into second and third periods. In these periods, each wrestler gets a turn to choose the starting position. They can start facing each other, or on top of their opponent, or under their opponent. If a wrestling match is tied after three periods, there are short **overtime** periods. At the end of the match, the wrestlers return to the center of the circle to shake hands again. The referee raises the hand of the winner and ends the match.

*A referee is in charge of the match. The referee gives points and **penalties**, and names the winner of the fight.*

Pin to win

The object of a folkstyle wrestling match is to pin your opponent to the mat. To win this way, a wrestler must hold his or her opponent's shoulders against the mat for two seconds in a row. This is called a fall or a pin. The fall must take place inside the large circle on the mat or it does not count. The referee slaps the mat to show that a **legal** fall has taken place.

This wrestler is pinning his opponent to win the match.

Bridges

One of the best ways to defend against a pin is to perform a neck bridge. To do a neck bridge, a wrestler arches their back and uses their head and feet to support their body weight. This technique lifts their shoulders off the mat so they cannot be pinned.

Game over

A fall ends the match right away. It does not matter what period it is or who was winning at the time of the fall. The wrestler who pinned down their opponent instantly wins the match.

Combos and cradles

There are hundreds of moves and pinning combinations wrestlers use to get falls.

A pinning combination is a hold that turns a wrestler so they can be pinned to the mat. One of the most common pinning combinations is the cradle. A cradle forces one or both of a wrestler's legs toward his or her head to trap the opponent on their back.

To perform a cradle, a wrestler moves above an opponent who is lying on his or her stomach.

The wrestler hooks one arm behind the opponent's knee. The wrestler wraps the other arm around the opponent's head, pulling the head back toward the trapped knee.

The wrestler then locks hands tightly together and lifts or rocks the opponent onto his or her back.

Half nelsons

Another popular pinning combination is the half nelson. A half nelson is used to turn your opponent from his or her stomach onto the back so they can be pinned. It can also be used to hold or control your opponent in an upright position.

The wrestler in blue is using a half nelson to control his opponent.

How to do it

To perform a half nelson, a wrestler moves behind the opponent or lies on the opponent's back. The wrestler puts one arm under the armpit of the opponent. The wrestler bends his or her own arm up and cups their hand on the back of the opponent's neck. The wrestler can then control the opponent or turn him or her over to pin them.

Full nelson

A full nelson is a hold in which a wrestler puts both arms under both armpits of the opponent and locks their hands on the opponent's neck. These dangerous holds are not allowed in folkstyle wrestling.

Get the point

Folkstyle wrestlers do not have to pin their opponents to win a match. They also earn points for controlling their opponents or escaping from them. Different wrestling moves earn different points. The wrestler who scores the most points takes the match.

A wrestler's points are displayed on a scoreboard like these.

Control and escape

Wrestlers earn points for controlling their opponents with near falls and reversals. A near fall occurs when a wrestler almost succeeds in pinning the opponent. A reversal is a move in which a wrestler rises from the mat and brings the opponent down in a single action.

Wrestlers also earn points for breaking free from their opponents. An escape is a move in which a wrestler gets out from under an opponent and turns to face him or her.

This wrestler is performing a stand-up escape. To do this move, a wrestler who is on the bottom gets on their hands and knees. He or she moves into a sitting position, then pushes off from the opponent and stands up.

Takedowns

Wrestlers also earn points for **takedowns**. A takedown is a move in which a wrestler brings a standing opponent down to the mat. Some takedowns target an opponent's head, arms, shoulders, or hips. In folkstyle wrestling, most takedowns attack an opponent's legs.

The single-leg takedown is a popular attack in folkstyle wrestling.

The wrestler on one knee is using a double-leg takedown to bring his opponent to the mat.

Double-leg takedown

One of the most common attacks is the double-leg takedown. This move is used when both wrestlers are standing. To perform a double leg, a wrestler dives toward the opponent's thighs. The wrestler uses their arms to pull on the opponent's legs. At the same time, the wrestler uses a shoulder to push on the opponent's stomach. A successful double leg throws the opponent off balance and sends him or her down to the mat.

Breaking the rules

Referees give penalty points for breaking the rules of folkstyle wrestling. Wrestlers get penalties for stalling, or leaving the mat during a match. They get penalties for swearing, kicking, hitting, scratching, choking, or biting their opponents. They also get penalties for performing dangerous moves or hurting their opponents on purpose.

This wrestler is performing an illegal move, or one that is not allowed in folkstyle wrestling.

A referee is watching these wrestlers to make sure they do not break any rules.

Kicked out

If wrestlers get too many penalty points, they are **disqualified** from the match. When wrestlers are disqualified, they are immediately taken out of the competition. Their opponent wins the match. Referees can also take wrestlers out of the match at any time for bad or dangerous behavior.

Meet your match

Young wrestlers compete at dual meets held at schools and clubs throughout the year. A dual meet is a match between two wrestling teams. One wrestler from each team competes in each weight class. The team with the most points at the end of the meet wins.

These wrestlers are competing for their schools at a university meet.

Tournaments

Wrestling teams also take part in tournaments. A tournament is an organized event that usually lasts for two or three days. Teams from near and far bring their best wrestlers to the mat. Individual wrestlers compete and earn points for winning matches. They also earn points for their teams. The wrestlers and teams with the most points at the end of the tournament take home the gold.

Fighting for gold

Wrestling is one of the world's oldest sports. It was practiced in ancient Greece and other places long ago. Greco-Roman wrestling was part of the first modern Olympic Games in 1896. Today, men compete in both Greco-Roman and freestyle events at the Olympics. Women compete in Olympic freestyle events. There are also events for many other wrestling styles and skill levels for men, women, and children around the world.

American Jordan Burroughs (in red) and Russian Denis Tsargush competed at the 2012 Olympic Games in London. Burroughs went on to win the gold.

Saori Yoshida celebrates a win in the women's freestyle event at the 2012 Olympic Games.

Wrestling champs

Russian Alexander Karelin is considered the greatest Greco-Roman wrestler of all time. He did not lose an international match—including the Olympics—in 13 years! American Bruce Baumgartner and Russian Alexander Medved are two of the best freestyle wrestlers ever to hit the mats. Japanese wrestlers Saori Yoshida and Kaori Ichohas have ruled the women's freestyle event. They won gold in their weight classes at the last three Olympic Games.

Flex your muscles

Wrestling is great exercise. It works muscles all over your body, especially your arms, legs, back, and neck. Wrestling also works your brain! You must stay alert and think quickly on the mat to win a wrestling match.

These wrestlers are flexing their muscles on the mats.

Find out more

If you want to flex your muscles and have some fun, contact your local wrestling club. Your school may have a wrestling club that you can join. If you have a brother or sister, you may have already done some wrestling at home!

These boys are working hard and having fun on the mats.

Glossary

Note: Boldfaced words that are defined in the text may not appear in the glossary.

disqualified No longer allowed to compete in a wrestling match

international Describes an event in which wrestlers from two or more countries compete

legal Allowed by the rules of wrestling

match A fight between two wrestlers

opponent Someone a wrestler competes against in a match

overtime Extra periods of time at the end of a wrestling match

penalty A punishment for breaking a rule

period A unit of time in a wrestling match

pin To hold a wrestler's shoulders down to the mat for two seconds to win a match

professional A person who is paid to play a sport or do a job

singlet A stretchy one-piece wrestling suit

takedown A move in which a wrestler attacks a standing opponent and brings them down to the mat

technique A skilled motion

weight class A group of wrestlers who are about the same size and weight

Index

Burroughs, Jordan Ernest 28
bridge 15
competition 25, 26, 28
cradle 16, 17
disqualification 25
dual meet 26
escape 21
fall 14, 15, 16
freestyle wrestling 6, 7
full nelson 19

Greco-Roman wrestling 6, 28, 29
half-nelson 18, 19
hold 4, 18
Karelin, Alexander 29
near fall 21
Olympics 6, 28, 29
penalty 13, 24, 25
pinning combination 16, 18
pin 4, 14, 15, 16, 18, 19, 20, 21

points 13, 20, 21, 22, 24, 25, 26, 27
professional wrestling 6
reversal 21
safety equipment 11
singlet 11
takedown 22, 23
team 26, 27
tournament 27
weight class 10, 26, 29
wrestling club 7, 31
Yoshida, Saori 29